William Giles Dix

Why a Catholic in the nineteenth century?

William Giles Dix

Why a Catholic in the nineteenth century?

ISBN/EAN: 9783742823113

Manufactured in Europe, USA, Canada, Australia, Japa

Cover: Foto ©Lupo / pixelio.de

Manufactured and distributed by brebook publishing software (www.brebook.com)

William Giles Dix

Why a Catholic in the nineteenth century?

WHY A CATHOLIC

IN THE

NINETEENTH CENTURY?

WILLIAM GILES DIX.

New York:
THE CATHOLIC PUBLICATION SOCIETY CO.,
9 BARCLAY STREET.
1878.

WHY A CATHOLIC

IN

THE NINETEENTH CENTURY?

LET us understand our words. Who is a Catholic? A Catholic is one who belongs to the Church of Christ, the Church which he proclaimed to be one, and one only, and which is called the Catholic Church, because designed to be the Church of all lands and of all ages until the end of the world.

What is the nineteenth century? It is an age which, inheriting the good and the ill of all preceding time, makes current and constant use of the inheritance. It is an age of intense energy. It is an age of wonderful material progress. The realm of nature is ransacked for discoveries of principles and of applications of principles for the need, comfort, or luxury of man. The realm of industry is ransacked for some new way to make a fortune or to spend one. It is an age of great intellectual excitement, but chiefly in the domain of natural science, which, not content with her proper position as the handmaid of intellectual, moral, and religious knowledge, is making a bold endeavor to usurp the throne of all science. It was once deemed and affirmed to be possible that science would in time dare to hold up a prism to the Divine Nature, to divide it into its component colors. That possibility has become a fact. A very noted lecturer, a sincere Christian believer, endeavors to explain the Divine Nature, in the interest of science, by holding up an intellectual prism to the eternal light and majesty of the Triune God. The endeavor is well intended, and I merely allude to it to show that even theological science, in some cases, obeys the triumphant demands of natural science, that the mysteries of the Deity and of the unseen universe of souls shall be explained, if explained at all, on the principles of natural science. Under the stormy surface of the nineteenth century there is, no doubt, a strong, deep current of religious faith; yet, so far as appears, this cannot be called an age of faith. Faith in divine and spiritual truth has, in this age, great potential forces and reserves, but they are held back, evidently to come forth, in God's way and hour, to subdue that haughty pretender, natural science, to her just condition as a subject, and to win back for religion her rightful crown and throne and sceptre as the sovereign of the realm of truth. The nineteenth century is an age remarkable for an attack on the citadel of Divine Truth all along the lines of the enemy. Worn-out weapons of assault have been made over anew, and entirely new weapons have been made with surpassing ingenuity, to besiege the throne of God and the divine origin and immortal destiny of man.

The nineteenth century is an age when governments as governments, and nations as nations, are trying to get as far away from God as possible; when materialism, coarse, sordid, unholy materialism, invades the cabinets of ministers and the thrones of kings; when to be a Christian statesman or a Christian ruler is, in the eyes of the world, to be a weak man, living in and for the past, blind to the duties of the present and the future. The nineteenth century is an age, of which the dominant and domineering characteristic is the worship of temporal advantage to the exclusion of eternal good, the placing of things seen and tangible in the room of things unseen and spiritual. In brief, the nineteenth century adopts and modifies the dogma of Mohammed, rejecting, however, that dogma's recognition of the Deity, and its controlling voice, swelling and sounding from the lofty minaret of intellectual pride, is, "There is no God but Nature; and Science is the only prophet of Nature."

Now, what has the Catholic Church to do with an age like this? She was well enough in the ages of barbarism, as representing intellectual and spiritual power working its way through souls of men little better than clods of earth; but of what use is the Catholic Church in the nineteenth century, when minds are illuminated with the concentrated intellectual splendor of so many ages? Of what use is the Catholic Church when everything in the universe, called divine or called human, must give an account of itself, why it is and what it is, or, failing to do so, go into the abyss of myths and fables? Of what use is the Catholic Church when minds are free, and printing is free, and speaking is free, and men are no longer slaves to worn-out ideas and worn-out institutions? Of what use is the Catholic Church when civilization has reached its highest point; when, if a man does not become rich and powerful, it is his own fault; when everybody gets along that deserves to get along; when poverty, voluntary or involuntary, is a crime, and success, however won, is a virtue? Of what use is the Catholic Church when books, books, books, magazines, newspapers, speeches of all kinds, are everywhere, keeping the minds of men busy, leading them into new paths of wonder, and when there is no need of standing still or of kneeling down, of saying prayers or chanting hymns like little children? Why should a free man kneel like a slave to acknowledge that there is or can be any greater being in the universe than man himself? What is the use of the Catholic Church in the nineteenth century, when man is sovereign in his own right, obeys no other authority, and needs no other authority, than his own will, requires no spur to action but his own interest, and asks for no other reward than his own satisfaction? The Catholic Church, perhaps, did some good in those dark old times when men needed a candle to see the way, and were thankful for it; but this nineteenth century is not night but day, bright glorious, dazzling day, shining with its own unborrowed light, shining all the time, and shining everywhere! When we have the sun of intellectual and material splendor, what is the need of the "dim, religious light" of the Catholic Church? The world has outgrown the Catholic Church; let her die, or be kept quietly and simply as an interesting relic of a by-gone order of civilization. Away with the Catholic Church! Let her get off the track of modern progress or be run over and torn in pieces. Such is the demand of the voices most powerful and most followed in the nineteenth century.

If the world has outgrown the Catholic Church, so much the worse for the world. But I deny it. Nearly nineteen centuries, crowded with the memories of Christians struggling, striving through all the troubles and woes of earthly life to win a title to immortal joy—striving against their own natures, striving against the enemies of their spiritual peace, striving against temptations and sins, striving on one side against foolhardy assurance and on the other against foolhardy despair, striving against their own weakness, striving against their own strength, striving against foes outside that besiege the soul or that try with stealthy cunning to undermine the soul, striving against traitors within the camp of the human heart in its life-long war—when nearly nineteen centuries bring forward their clouds of witnesses crowded with the experiences of Christian history and of the Christian life, then may we well believe that, while human beings are human beings, the world cannot outgrow the Catholic Church. Men have souls to be saved in the nineteenth as in the first century. Times may differ, modes of warfare may differ, weapons of attack and defence may differ, but through all the changes of time human souls are human soldiers fighting for salvation, as they must continue to fight; and how can they better maintain the conflict than by being armed with the celestial graces of that Church which the Saviour of men appointed as the guide and defender of men through the dangerous wilderness of life, and through the yet more dangerous gardens of life to the Paradise of God?

I speak not now to those who deny God, Christ, or some kind of Christian Church, but to those who, while believing that they ought to be Christians, see no reason why they should be Catholics. Well, there is no reason why Christians should be Catholics in the nineteenth century, if there was no reason why they should be Catholics in the first century; but if there was a reason why Christians should be Catholics in the first century, that reason avails and is binding in the nineteenth century, unless it can be clearly proved that the obligation has been annulled by the same authority which imposed it. Was there such an obligation in the first century? To prove this point I have no need to refer to any of the great Fathers of the Church, to sacred or profane history, to councils after the apostolic times, or to papal decrees. I hold that the New Testament, and the Protestant version of that, proves these propositions:

I. Christ founded a Church.

II. Christ founded one Church, one only; not a corporation of national churches, not a federal union of churches, but literally one Church.

III. That one Church of Christ was intended to be the only spiritual guide, on earth, of Christians.

IV. That Church had the promise of endurance and of guidance until the end of the world.

V. That Church was the beginning of the Church known historically as the Catholic Church..

1st. Christ founded a Church. This is hardly denied by any Christians, even the Quakers holding to something like an organization or institution. Nor did Christ, in founding his Church, annul the Jewish Church. He expanded it, and made it the Church of the whole world instead of the Church of one people, and he did so by the right and power of his Incarnation; and he enjoined on the adherents of his Church, so changed in spirit and extent, the truths and practices growing out of the fact of the Incarnation. I quote the words of Christ to Peter, not to consider the primacy, but simply the fact that they speak of the Church: "Thou art Peter, and upon this rock I will build my Church" (Matthew xvi. 18). The apostles always take for granted the central fact that Christ founded a Church. They do not set to work to prove it; they take it for granted, which is the highest proof. St. Paul says to the Corinthians: "And God hath set some in the Church, first apostles," etc. (1 Corinth. xii. 28). To the Ephesians he writes (Eph. i. 22, 23), declaring that God the Father "hath put all things under his feet [the feet of

Christ], and gave him to be the head over all things to the Church, which is his body, the fulness of him that filleth all in all." Christ, then, founded a Church.

2d. Christ founded one Church, one only; not a corporation of national churches, not a federal union of churches, but literally one Church. The very words quoted above prove this. Christ says: "my Church." It is impossible that he could mean by "my Church," a church in Judea, another in Greece, another in Italy, another in Spain—a church or churches in every province of the Roman Empire, and subsequently in other parts of the world, becoming national churches, each independent of the rest, and united only by a vague kind of fellowship—for in this passage he says: "Thou art Peter, and upon this rock I will build my Church." I am not now insisting upon the Catholic authority of Peter. In this passage I quote the words because they prove from the very lips of our divine

Lord that he founded one Church, and one only. He could not have meant churches independent entirely each of the others, agreeing only, and perhaps not agreeing, in certain dogmas; for these independent churches could not be one church. He could not have meant a federal union of churches, for how could a federal union of churches be founded on a rock—on one rock? On one rock could only be founded one church. Those who maintain that our Lord founded a series or succession of national churches, or a federal union of churches, must prove that each church was founded on a rock of its own. This they cannot do. It is but just to say that they do not pretend to do it. They try to destroy, by illogical interpretation, the power of that one rock. They try to get that one rock out of the way, but there it stands; there it has stood for nearly nineteen centuries; there it will stand until the end of the world. It makes not the slightest difference, in this case, whether you adopt the Protestant interpretation that the *rock* refers to the confession of Peter, or the Catholic interpretation that *rock* refers to the representative authority of Peter. In either case the *rock* stands as the foundation, not of a number of churches, but of one Church, whose power and authority reach throughout the world, but having one foundation, and one only.

The apostles, indeed, address the church at Corinth, the churches in Galatia, and so on, as St. John, in the Revelation, writes to the seven churches of Asia; and in the Acts of the Apostles it is said that St. Paul went, confirming the churches. There is no confusion here. These are not churches independent of each other. They are different members of one body, just as the apostles themselves, separate as individuals, were one sacred society, appointed and ordained by Christ. They were no more separate or independent churches, as far as authority was concerned, than Catholic churches now in the same city are. They were all portions of that one Church which was founded on one rock. They never sought or desired to be anything else. It was their glory and their pride that they were nothing else. They all formed, however distant from each other, one loving and living communion of believers, members of one holy Church of Christ, drawing their divine authority from one source, obeying one guide, sustained by one altar, and looking forward to one Paradise of eternal rest. Now, if a federal union of churches did not exist by divine authority, in the times of the apostles, it could not be expected to exist later by divine authority. But a large portion of the Protestant world will not admit even so low an idea of the Church of Christ, as its being a federal union of churches. They disclaim, disavow, and denounce any relation or connection of any kind with the one Church, the one, and the only one, historical Church which avows its own original unity. They boast of their separation and independence. They have seceded outright and take pride in the secession. By their own rule of faith, however—the Bible, and the Bible alone—I have shown that Christ founded one Church, and one only. If it was a part of the divine arrangement respecting the Christian Church that at any future time it should be divided, there ought to be some intimation of such a divine permission in the New Testament. Where is it? You cannot find that intimation or permission or command anywhere. You cannot find anything which can be tortured into such an intimation, permission, or command. On the contrary, you find passages which indicate that the power of the Christian Church will increase in time; but you cannot find a trace or a shadow of any kind or degree of inference that the organic unity of the Christian Church can ever be broken up like a ship wrecked on a rocky shore or by a tornado on the high seas. The full organic authority of the Christian Church was not thoroughly developed in the apostolic times, for the need had not come; but the divine order, the divine principles, the divine theory, waiting to be developed by the growth and expansion of the Church, existed, and we need not go one inch beyond the letter of the New Testament to find them. I have shown that Christ founded a Church, that he founded one Church; and if there can be found any word recorded as spoken by Christ or his apostles, showing it to be a part of the divine plan that that Church of Christ should ever be divided into many churches, each retaining the graces promised to the Church of Christ, let that word be pointed out. The challenge may be safely made that whenever the apostles allude to the Church, unless the word be qualified by the name of a place, in the Sacred Scriptures, they mean exactly what Christ himself meant by the Church —one undivided, indivisible body of his faithful ones through all the earth; and that whenever they allude to a church or to churches, naming a place or places, they mean only, and cannot mean anything else than, as it were, a family or families in one and the same, the very same, Christian empire of faith throughout the world.

3d. That one Church of Christ was intended to be the only spiritual guide, on earth, of Christians. Our Lord said that, if all personal efforts of reconciliation fail in a case of offence, then "tell it unto the Church: but, if he neglect to hear the Church, let him be unto thee as a heathen man and a publican"; and he adds: "Verily I say unto you, whatsoever ye shall bind on earth shall be bound in heaven; and whatsoever ye shall loose on earth shall be loosed in heaven" (Matthew xviii. 17, 18). It would seem to be impossible for words to be found more decisive of the spiritual and binding authority of an institution than these words of Christ.

I do not insist upon the meaning which all Catholics give to the latter words of this passage, though that meaning seems to be an imperative and logical one; but I quote the words to show that the authority, whatever it may be, is a spiritual authority, otherwise its exercise on earth would not be ratified in heaven. It is a comprehensive authority, for it says, "whatever ye shall bind" and "whatever ye shall loose," showing that the commission included not only offences between man and man, but offences of which man was guilty in his relation to God. It is the authority of the Church of Christ, for He Himself speaks; he names the Church —His Church, as it must be—as the arbiter, the final arbiter, of offences between man and man, as Christians, yielding submission to the authority of the Church, or, if not yielding submission, to be cast out. It is a delegated authority, for Christ speaks in this way to his disciples, and to the disciples as representing the Church—for that the connection positively requires; not as individuals, not merely as Christians, but as having authority in the Church of Christ, communicated by himself. This commission regarding offences not only of man towards man, but of man towards God, was so understood and practised by the Apostles during their lives and labors. Peter condemned Ananias and Saphira, "and great fear came upon all the Church, and upon as many as heard these things" (Acts v. 11).

When a dispute arose about the binding force of the Mosaic law on the Gentile converts, the whole question, by the consent of all, was referred to a council of the Church, and the decision was accepted as sacred and irrevocable; yet the decision was rendered in words which, if not true, if not known to be true by the apostles and elders assembled in the council and holding authority from Christ, who had ascended to heaven, would be nothing more nor less than blasphemous. These are their words: "For it seemed good to the Holy Ghost and to us" (Acts xv. 28). We must, then, believe that the Church of Christ had authority, and, if it had, it has authority, to decide questions of religious faith and discipline ; or we must believe that the apostles—those whom Christ had chosen, and to whom he gave his holy commission when about to ascend to heaven, including Matthias, who had been afterwards chosen, and Paul, who had been miraculously converted to the faith which he had tried to destroy—that these, the humblest of men, meek as lambs in all that concerned themselves, but the boldest of men, courageous as lions in declaring and exercising the authority of God in Christ committed to their charge—that these men were guilty of direct and positive blasphemy in attributing to the Holy Ghost their own human decision. Will you believe that the Church, in the council at Jerusalem, exercised her rightful authority over Christians in respect to spiritual discipline and obedience, and, if rightful authority then, may exercise it now; or will you believe that St. Peter, St. Paul, St. James, and the rest were guilty of exactly the same sin—rebellious assumption of divine rights—which drove Lucifer and his mutinous crew from the heights of heaven to the depths of hell? Are you willing to believe this? Of course you are not; but that you must believe, or believe that the Church of Christ, the one Church of Christ, the only one Church of Christ, had spiritual jurisdiction over all that professed the name of Christ; and if she had it once, she has it now. You will not charge blasphemy against the apostles of our Lord. Such a sin cannot be suspected without a fatal injury to the Christian faith. What Church, then, was that so miraculously endowed? By the consent of all, it was the Christian Church, for it could not have been any other; it was the Apostolic Church, for it could not have been any other; it was the only Church then existing, for there was but one; and if that one Church, that only one, that Apostolical Church, that Church of Christ, was not the nucleus of that Church which is now seen and known in all lands under the sun, and which all men call the Catholic Church, will any Christian, Pagan, Jew, Catholic, Protestant, Greek, Turk, or Infidel say what church it was and must have been? And if it was the Catholic Church, doing its great work on earth, it once had wonderful gifts and prerogatives from God; if it had them once, it has them now, unless there has been a new revelation recalling and annulling those gifts and prerogatives, unless God has again become incarnate in human form, and by his living voice has abrogated the Christian dispensation. The Jewish Church was merged in the Christian Church as a consequence of the Incarnation and by the authority of God Incarnate. That is recorded in the Revelation of our Lord and Saviour Jesus Christ.

Now, if there has been another revelation, where is it? No man in the wide world ever heard of it. Where is it? If God has abrogated the Christian Church and taken away her authority, when did he do it? how did he do it? Where is the record of his doing it? If another church exists by divine right, superseding the Apostolic Church, the continuous and historical Church of Christ, let that church show her divine credentials, for nothing else will do. One Church, and one only, can be traced through all the ages to the Council at Jerusalem, to the day of Pentecost, to the Mount of Ascension. The whole world knows what Church that is. The New Testament, the Protestant version, proves that that Church once had spiritual jurisdiction over all Christians. If she has lost that jurisdiction, when did she lose it, why, and how? In a matter of such importance to the souls of men we must insist on knowing the time, the place, and the circumstances. Let it also be noted that the decision of the Council at Jerusalem was regarded by all Christians, however earnest may have been their debates, as completely and for ever closing the question. And, literally, no more is heard of the dispute. Why? Because it was no longer a dispute, but a case settled.

I have suggested some of the difficulties which are made by human caprice alone, because it will not take the plain meaning of plain words, and tries to darken words that are as plain as the noon-day sun, which tries to resolve into thin air historical and spiritual truth which is as firm as a rock.

4th. That Church had the promise of endurance and of guidance until the end of the world. All, of course, on this point that we can expect to find in the New Testament is the promise that the Church should so endure, and that we do find: "Then the eleven disciples went away into Galilee, into a mountain which Jesus had appointed them. And when they saw him, they worshipped him; but some doubted. And Jesus came and spoke unto them, saying, All power is given unto me in heaven and in earth. Go ye therefore, and teach all nations, baptizing them in the name of the Father, and of the Son, and of the Holy Ghost, teaching them to observe all things whatever I have commanded you; and lo, I am with you alway, even unto the end of the world" (Matthew xxviii. 16-20).

Sometimes, in the Sacred Scriptures, a single word has an intensity of meaning which a careless reader may entirely miss. It is so here. The single word *therefore* has just such an intensity of meaning. Our Lord says: "All power is given unto me in heaven and in earth. Go ye *therefore*"—that is, because all power is mine, because I am to exercise it on earth while earth shall last, go ye *therefore*, and teach all nations. For the very reason that ye represent me, teach to the world what I have taught you; "And lo! I am with you alway, even unto the end of the world." This means, and can only mean, the end of the world in time, not in space. The original word cannot be tortured to mean anything else. If this commission is not a commission for men, who, as representing Christ, to whom is given all power in heaven and in earth, are to exercise throughout the world, until the end of the world, the authority which they had derived from him, what can it mean? But the disciples to whom these words were spoken were mortal men; they must die; they did die; yet the power, the prerogative, and the obligation remained—where? In that church which Christ instituted; for the command was to these men in their apostolical character, and their apostolical character consisted in their being rulers, guides, and teachers of the Church of God. If these things are not so, then say how they are. If plain words cannot speak plain, then make them plain and say what they mean.

"Teach all nations, baptizing them in the name of the Father, and of the Son, and of the Holy Ghost." Of course the nations are to be baptized as individuals. In this case the people constitute the nations; yet there is also the idea that nations, as nations, are to be made Christian. But what can it mean, to teach and baptize all nations, if not to make the people that compose them members of the Christian Church? I do not refer to the universal interpretation of baptism by the Church, by all the sects of Christendom, which consider the rite as binding, as introducing to the Christian community, except to disclaim such reference as an argument; for, at present, I am trying to prove, by the words of Scripture alone, the unity, jurisdiction, and enduring power of the Christian Church. I make the challenge that the New Testament, and the Protestant version—the Protestant rule of faith, taken entirely apart from any subsequent interpretations or comments—sup-

ports the Catholic theory of the Church of
Christ. Look at the plain words quoted;
compare them with others in the New Testament, and make no reference to ecclesiastical history; imagine, for the moment,
nearly nineteen centuries blotted out, and,
if the plain words do not mean that the
apostles are commanded to teach and to
baptize all nations—that is, the people of
all nations—and by so doing to make them
members of the Church of Christ, what do
those words mean? And if this be so—
and it cannot be otherwise—what was the
Christian Church, if not the same which
all the world now calls the Catholic
Church? If Christ our Lord founded two
or more churches—in plain contradiction
to his own words, "my Church"— then
prove it, and prove it by the Protestant
"rule of faith," if you can. No performer in a circus ever underwent more contortions and distortions, or more gyrations or
dislocations, than people have to undergo
who twist the holy words, "my Church,"

to mean fifty or a hundred churches, more or less.

5th. That Church was the beginning of the Church known historically as the Catholic Church—that is, the Church of all lands and of all ages. The commission of our Lord to the apostles proves and promises the Catholicity of the Church in time and space; but I have made this proposition a separate one, in order to show that in the apostolical times the Catholicity of the Church was not a mere ideal design of the then future ages, but that it actually began as a practical result, application, and illustration of the teaching of Christ and of his institution of his Church.

In the second chapter of the Acts of the Apostles is recorded the wonderful visitation of the Spirit of God at Pentecost. On that day began the Catholicity of the Christian Church, divinely manifesting to all the world the authority and benediction of a divine institution.

Though the apostles were Jews, yet those who heard them preach, coming from very different regions, understood them by a miracle of divine grace. "Parthians, and Medes, and Elamites, and the dwellers in Mesopotamia, and in Judea, and Cappadocia, in Pontus, and Asia, Phrygia, and Pamphylia, in Egypt, and in the parts of Libya about Cyrene, and strangers of Rome, Jews and proselytes, Cretes and Arabians, we do hear them speak in our tongues the wonderful works of God" (Acts ii. 9-10). In the end of the chapter it says: "And the Lord added to the Church daily such as should be saved." The Catholic version says: "And the Lord increased daily together such as should be saved"; but the meaning is the same, for both versions agree in recording the baptism of all who were converted. If this Church to which believers were added about eighteen hundred and forty years ago—believers from so many different regions—was not the same Church which in the year 1877 we call the Catholic Church, what church was it ? On the day of Pentecost was represented and proved the Catholicity in extent of the Catholic Church. It prefigured the time when all nations should become Christian. That great result has not yet been reached, but it is coming. More glorious "ages of faith" are yet to be than ever yet have been; yet all the spiritual victories of the Church through all coming time until the end of time will be nothing more, however glorious and consoling, than the continuation of that triumphant hour when the Catholicity of the Church of Christ was proclaimed by tongues of fire from heaven.

The record of no family on earth can be so clearly traced as the record of that great Christian family, the Catholic Church, through all the centuries of her existence. Christ promised to be with the representatives of his Church until the end of time. Prove that that promise has been broken; prove that it has been annulled; or, if you sincerely believe in your Saviour-God and in his divine promise, that cannot fail; then kneel in loyalty and love, and acknowledge that the Church which now appears to the view of men in many a glittering cross crowning many a holy altar is the same Church which, ages ago, appeared to the view of men in many a living flame. Did the Church of Christ after a few years subside into the ground like a river that disappears in the sands? It did not. It continued. It continues. It will continue until the end of the world—the same Church, the same one Church, the same Church of Christ, the same Catholic Church, which received her divine commission from the lips of our Lord, which began her divine work under that commission, as a Catholic Church, when cloven tongues of fire were signs and seals of the presence of the Holy Ghost.

The Church was one and has remained one. Branches have been broken off, but the trunk of that Catholic tree has never been divided. The Church had the promise of universality; she has become universal. There is no land beneath the sun, hardly an island in the most lonely sea, that has not felt the pressure of a Catholic kneeling at his devotions. The Church had the promise of endurance; she has endured for nearly nineteen hundred years. She has endured, unshaken by tornadoes of human rage; she has endured, though traitors have betrayed her and though nations have besieged her; she has endured through the weakness of mortal man, endowed with divine prerogatives; she has endured through thunders and lightnings that have blasted empires and scattered crowns and sceptres like leaves. She has endured when royal dynasties have died as though smitten by the plague; when palaces, seeming as strong as the everlasting hills, have crumbled to dust; she has endured while around the rock on which she stood earthquakes of civil strife have yawned and have devoured mighty towers of defence and mighty armies of assault; she has endured in spite of all that the powers of darkness could teach or do; she has endured because under her feet has been the rock of ages, because on her head has been the helmet of salvation, because in her hand has been the sword of the Holy Spirit, because ever sounding in her ear and confirming her strength have been the words of her Saviour-God, "The gates of hell shall not prevail." She has endured; she will endure until the world itself shall die—until? She will endure through the wreck of time and through the flames of burning worlds. The Catholic Church will never die; out of the ruins of a universe she will spring, translated to enjoy the vision of God in the new heaven and earth which shall never fade or fall.

I think I have proved the five propositions. Let me say, besides, the Catholic Church is in possession. She has been in possession for nearly nineteen centuries; there is no reason, judging from the analogies of her history, that she will not be in possession for nineteen centuries more, if the world shall last so long. If the Catholic Church is wrongfully in possession, turn her out, but first prove the fact. The Catholic Church is not an Irish tenant, to be ejected from her own freehold by the caprice of a tyrant or a pettifogger's writ. First prove your right to turn her out. That is hard work, as many have found. After proving or asserting your right to turn her out, then you must try to do it; and that you will find to be very hard work. Whole nations have tried before now to turn out the Catholic Church—to turn her out of the world. They have advanced in battle array to do it; but, overpowered by her divine majesty, they have knelt at her feet to crave her pardon, and to bathe with tears of penitence and joy the very hands which they intended to cover with blood. What has happened once will happen again. There is many a Saul in Catholic history who has become the rival of Paul in zeal to build up what he tried to break down. In trying to turn out the Catholic Church what do you do? You deny the right of the King of Glory, our Lord and Saviour, to his earthly throne; you deny his own words, which could not have been spoken without a meaning: "All power is given unto me in heaven and in earth."

The Catholic Church is Christ himself leading, teaching, warning, consoling men in their earthly journey. Civilization never yet has outgrown the Church. On the contrary, the higher the civilization, the more the Church is needed, aside from the fact that no institution has ever done so much for true civilization as the Catholic Church; but civilization without religion tends to the most defiant, corrupt, demoralized condition of society that can be imagined. Talk of wild beasts and savages! The wildest and most destructive of wild beasts are men without the sense of religious responsibility, when possessed by the devil of intellectual pride, of social disorder, of ungodly ambition, of political ruin, though they may speak the most polite language, though they may be arrayed with faultless taste. Such savages may exist even in Catholic countries—savages who rebel consciously and wilfully against all the ennobling, refining, purifying influences of the Church, and so, by a natural as well as supernatural law, become worse from the very means designed to make them better.

Who murdered the Archbishop of Paris and his faithful companions a few years ago? The vile wretches who actually did the deed were but instruments. The real authors of that crime were the atheistical, sentimental, polite, patriotic savages who wore the finest cloth, whose white hands were covered with the daintiest kid, whose presence flashed with gems, and who could talk about the rights of man with power and eloquence. During the French Revolution some of the men who sent daily to the guillotine, with exultation and joy, aged men and quiet matrons, blooming youths and maidens, could fill hours with their glowing periods about the blessedness of human equality, the virtue of benignant charity, and the beauty of patriotic devotion. Let us have the lions and tigers fresh and furious from their native jungles before the human lions and human tigers, with velvet touch and glossy look and outward smiles, that in times of civil commotion are made ferocious by their rebellion against the law of God, social order, and Christian civilization.

Why a Catholic in the nineteenth century? Because this age especially needs the compass of divine and immutable truth. It is an age when the fountains of the great deep of opinion are broken up. It is an age of stormy debates and conflicts on the principles of things. Rebellion against the laws of the Christian faith and of the Christian Church has burst like a storm at sea. Christian civilization is battling like a ship against the combined furies of barbarism, infidelity, scorn, and malignant hate. It is just such a time when the compass must be closely and constantly watched. Where is the compass of Christian civilization? It is in the care, and only in the care, of the Catholic Church. Through ages of conflict the needle of that compass has pointed directly and persistently to that north star, the bright, unwavering, eternal law of God. So it points now; so it will point for ever. Distorted minds of men, apostate nations, hostile societies, parliaments, and pulpits ungratefully conspire to destroy the noble ship which is guided by the compass of eternal law and is freighted with immortal destinies. I said *ungratefully*, and with good reason. Protestantism has not a single treasure, social, civil, or religious, which is worth keeping or defending for an hour, which she did not get from or through the Catholic Church. Ay, many a scholar who rails at the Catholic Church as the enemy of knowledge, has drawn his weapons of attack from the precious armories of the very Church which he assails; and but for her earnest and incessant care in opening the fountains, and in widening and deepening the streams of knowledge, would himself be no wiser or better than a Patagonian savage.

The great ocean of time is strewn with wrecks of nations, drifting, drifting, drifting, going anywhere and bound nowhere. Blasted by lightning, conquered by foes, overturned by the beating sea or by beating whirlwinds, they float, if they float at all, rudderless, aimless, hopeless, deserted and bare. One ship has survived every storm. One ship has drawn harmless the lightning and hushed the voice of the thunder. One ship has never turned from her course. One ship has kept her compass, her rudder, her pilot, her faithful crew; and that ship is the Catholic Church. Through all the besieging ages one stronghold has never surrendered; it is the Catholic Church. On the great battle-field of history there is one banner which has never fallen into the dust, and that is the banner of the Catholic Church, the banner of the Holy Cross and of the Holy Dove. Would the nations partake of the enduring power of the Catholic Church? Then on their banners let the star of Bethlehem shine brightest and farthest; let the Holy Dove there spread her benignant wings, and on their ample folds let the Holy Cross be interwoven, the symbol of him who is the only Saviour of nations, as he is the only Saviour of men.

I have spoken as though it were merely a question of choice to be a Catholic—on the whole best, but not a binding duty. No Catholic will have misunderstood me.

I affirm boldly and without reserve that it is the duty of every believer in Christ to be a Catholic. I affirm that every professing Christian, outside the Catholic Church, plainly disobeys the command of that very Saviour on whom he relies for salvation. I can prove it, and I will. Not a word can be found in the New Testament, spoken by our Lord or by any of his disciples, sanctioning the belief that at any future time the unity of the Church could be rightfully broken, that a division of the Christian Church into various denominations was a part of the divine plan when the Christian Church was founded. On the contrary, every word spoken by our Lord or by any of his disciples is plainly, directly, solemnly against any such possible sanction. Divisions were foretold, but in every instance they were spoken of as departures from the faith. If ever anything like what we call a denomination was referred to by the apostles, it was only to be denounced as treason to the faith, order, and discipline of the Church of Christ. Not one instance can be found where separation from the Church was deemed a possible remedy for any alleged injustice committed by those who had the right to rule in the Church. If any disorders should occur, they were to be corrected in the Church and by the Church. "All denominations of the Christian Church"—what could St. Peter and St. Paul have made of that phrase, so common now? They would not have known what to make of it. They use, I admit, the word "brethren" in speaking of those who cause divisions, but they prefix a word which defines the meaning: they call them "false brethren." That is not praise, but censure.

So far is carried this inculcation of unity by our Lord and his disciples that you cannot find that he or they ever urged even Jewish believers in Christ to separate from the Jewish Church. Our Lord denounced the rulers of that church, but nevertheless required obedience to them. It should never be forgotten that the Church of Christ superseded the Jewish Church, not by destroying it, but by enlarging it; not by making divisions in it, but by expanding its gifts. Its ceremonies were superseded, but its moral law was made more stringent and binding. Even its sacrifice was not taken away; only the sign yielded, when God's hour had come, to the thing signified. Believers in Christ were cast out of the synagogues, but they did not go out voluntarily. Christ never enjoined schism, even towards the Jewish Church. No doubt the change from the Jewish to the Christian dispensation was a stupendous revolution; but it was a revolution brought about according to God's eternal providence and by the direct authority of God Incarnate. This mighty revolution was brought about by the absorption, not by the destruction, of the Jewish Church. The promise was made that the Christian Church, so absorbing the Jewish, should be one ; and one Church, as regards the vast majority of Christian believers, it has remained for nearly nineteen centuries. Of one Church only on earth can that fact be affirmed, and that is the Catholic Church. We have a right to conclude, we are compelled to conclude, that schism, as a cure for any possible disorder in discipline, for any demerit of any individuals, was never designed by our Lord, but was positively forbidden. Why? Because there could be no greater disorder or demerit than schism itself. Unworthy members were, indeed, cast out of the Church ; others in the Church were condemned, submitted, and were pardoned; but for the greater part of the time from the day of Pentecost to this moment the vast majority of Christian believers in the world have been members of the Catholic Church. Consider also this point: the Catholic Church is accused by her enemies of being very corrupt. By some very sincere people she is believed to be very corrupt. Now, for the moment I am not going to combat that accusation; but I call your attention to this fact: through all this alleged corruption the Catholic Church has lived and still lives. Now, one might infer from this very fact that the corruption could not be so great as charged; but take it the other way—if the Catholic Church has survived all this corruption; if she is now stronger in numbers, relative to the whole world, than ever before; if her people were never more loyal than now, even when governments have proved false to her service, is it not right to believe that there is a divine principle in the Catholic Church which no faults of individuals can destroy? Is it not a striking fulfilment of our Lord's promise, that the gates of hell should not prevail, that the Catholic Church has proved, for so many centuries, triumphant not only over foes without, but foes within? that she has survived not only the assaults of enemies, but also the work of "false brethren"?

There has never been but one Catholic Church—only one Church, so named, everywhere. We hear of Old Catholics; we hear of Reformed Catholics; some of our Anglican friends like to call the ecclesiastical department of the British Government a branch of the Catholic Church; but the single designation, the Catholic Church, is claimed by one Church only and conceded to one Church only throughout the world. Even the Greeks do not claim to be Catholics; to this day they do not dare to claim the name of Catholics. One Church only has a claim to have an unbroken continuity from the apostolic times, and that is the Catholic Church. You may say that the old Church was allowed to keep the name, but the great evils which had grown up in her history required to be corrected; there was no disposition to correct them; and, consequently, separation was justifiable. I deny that point-blank. Separation was not justifiable, unless you can prove from

the words of Christ that separation was to
be a remedy for any disorders in the
Church—that is, separation from the Church
by the voluntary action of any of its members; separation of unworthy members by
the Church was, of course, a part of its
discipline. Notwithstanding these evils
which you denounce, the Church has remained one. A candid enemy of the Catholic Church must admit that its good
has immeasurably exceeded the evil which,
as an institution administered by mortal
man, it may in some of its manifestations
have contracted. The greater you make
the faults of individuals in the Catholic
Church, the more you denounce the ambition of this or that pontiff, the stronger
you make the argument for the divine
origin of a Church which could withstand
so many faults and so much ambition.
If you outside the Catholic Church are so
good, so saintly, so upright, so faithful
toward God and man, why not give the
Catholic Church the benefit of your supe-

rior sanctity, so as to reform her abuses? The worse you make out the Catholic Church to be, the worse her endurance makes out your conduct to be in professing to be Christians while refusing to be Catholics; for the Catholic Church had a divine origin. All Christians will admit that, even if some accuse her of departing from the faith. But if she had a divine origin, no other church could have had a divine origin; for there was but one Church, and, if there was but one Church, there is but one Church, and that Church has a right to the allegiance of all Christian people; and that Church is the Catholic Church, for it cannot be any other.

Will you say that the Catholic Church is a dead Church—that it lives only a kind of galvanic life, and, consequently, has no claim on the loyalty of living Christians? Well, if the Catholic Church be really dead, God be thanked for that death in life which provides for so many of the poor, the sick, and the sorrowful, which leads so many myriads of mortals through the perilous toils and pains of life, and through the yet more perilous pleasures and leisures of life, guides them gently to the borders of the grave, dismisses them into eternity with prayers and benedictions, and, when all that is mortal is laid out of sight, continues to pray for their departed souls. The Catholic Church is not dead. How can she die, being daily invigorated by the water of life which she draws from the well of eternal truth, by the bread of life which came down from heaven, and which she alike receives and bestows, and by the light of life which shines for ever from the throne of God?

The Catholic Church is not dying or likely to die. She lives to do her work. What is that work? It is to conquer the world for Christ. By what authority? That of Christ himself. There can be no higher, no more binding authority. These propositions confirm alike the right and the duty of every Christian to be a loyal member of the Catholic Church. The Catholic Church is a great spiritual army, aggressive, unyielding, determined, armed with the gifts of God, ordered and resolute to obey the command of Christ, to baptize all nations, to make the law of God in Christ the law of men and the law of nations. Christian obedience is everywhere taught in the New Testament. There is not a word or a line that can justify a Christian in deserting the great army whose design is the spiritual conquest of the world. Lord Nelson made the signal flash through his fleet: "England expects every man to do his duty." With far greater significance the signal flashes through the Christian world: Christ expects every man to do his duty, and to do it as he has appointed by the way of the Catholic Church. How can a man be true to God and his Church, if he refuses to join the army of God and his Church? The world so far has been conquered for Christ by his Church appointed for that end—an organization, wise, yet aggressive and fearless, in which dwells, and has dwelt since the day of Pentecost, the living, teaching, directing power of the Holy Ghost. What has thus far been the rule will continue to be the rule, until literally and truly the world shall be converted to Christ.

God forbid that any Catholic should be unwilling to acknowledge the earnest sincerity with which vast numbers of Protestants hold their faith and try to promote and extend it, meaning truly to serve the Saviour of men; but—not here to speak of their neglecting a positive duty—they are spending their strength unwisely. They fail to make that deep and enduring impression which so much energy and sincerity under Catholic direction could not fail to secure. The Captain of our salvation requires and commands that all who profess to be his soldiers should be in the ranks of his glorious army—the grand army of holiness against sin, of faith against unbelief, of order against disorder, of celestial graces against earthly corruptions, of heaven against hell. Are mutineers loyal to their captain, or even those who by no means intend to be mutinous, who nevertheless act in the spirit of disobedience to the Church which Christ has commissioned to guide in his stead? Are they who disobey the command of unity able to obey the command of conquest which depends on that unity?

Protestant brethren—you who desire, pray for, and strive for that precious gift of grace, a soul on fire with the love of Christ, with his love for you, with your love for him—can you reasonably desire, pray for, and strive for that priceless treasure, whilst you make all kinds of excuses for remaining outside that great communion, the corner-stone of which was laid by the divine hand of that very Redeemer whom you aim and try to love and to serve? You say that the Catholic Church has usurped prerogatives, and that this usurpation annuls your obligation of loyalty. Beware how you reason on that point, lest after all what you call usurpation shall prove to be nothing more than the exercise and application of powers and gifts existing from the beginning. Can you believe that Christ himself did not foresee and provide for the extension of his earthly kingdom—the Catholic Church—and, if so, that he also provided the powers requisite to govern that kingdom when it should literally include all nations? How is it with mechanical forces? The more you extend the belts and wheels of your machinery, the more you must increase the central power. The wider the Catholic Church grows, the stronger must she grow at the centre of unity; yet this is not done by any new creation of forces, simply by the application of forces already potentially existing. The Catholic Church has never exercised any powers, she has never claimed any powers, she never will claim any powers, that are not direct and logical deductions from the very words of Christ. Of course all Catholics believe that the Church is the larger circle which includes the Scriptures; nevertheless, in all the debates and treatises of centuries about the prerogatives of the Church, the main intent has been to find out historically and logically, What did Christ himself order and appoint? A word is in many mouths—*ultramontane*—intended to represent extreme views of papal rights. Now, I care not whom you select among the defenders of the powers of St. Peter and his successors, you will find the attributes ascribed by any such writer to the successors of St. Peter not so strong as the single commission of our Lord to his apostles recorded in the New Testament. The most ultramontane writers that I know of are Matthew, Mark, Luke, and John. The only difficulty which any one finds in the interpretation of the words of our Lord referring to his Church is because those words are so plain and direct. They so clearly set forth the amplest prerogatives ever claimed for the Church of Christ that many people seem to believe that they cannot mean what they seem to mean, and, therefore, must be explained away.

Protestant believers in Christ! you are wasting your energies in a guerilla warfare, if not in actual mutiny. In the Catholic Church you will be working in harmony with the plans of God from all eternity. You will there find an ample field for all the various powers with which God has endowed you. Are you orators? Where are more sublime themes for your eloquence than the glories of the Christian Church, the glories of the Gospel of grace and salvation adapted by her ministrations to every want of the souls of men? Are you philosophers? The noblest system of philosophy which the world has ever known is the plan of redemption and its attendant truths that cluster around it like stars around a central sun. The deepest thinkers have not sounded the depth of that divine philosophy. The loftiest thoughts have not soared to its highest height. Are you poets? Christianity can entrance your souls with holier visions, with more impressive mysteries, than seer or sibyl ever sang. In power to move the heart and refine and exalt the imagination, to set forth figures of divine beauty and grandeur before the minds of men, Parnassus yields to Calvary, and the Nine Muses to the innumerable choirs of saints and angels around the eternal throne. Are you painters or sculptors or architects? Catholic art, and Catholic art only, has built upon earth structures as firm as the rock on which they stand, yet as aerial in beauty as if they were about to soar into the air; in which "thoughts that wander through eternity" seem at home, where worship seems spontaneous and intuitive, and religion an instinct of the soul. Where, except in Catholic art, will you see portrayed the sorrows and the triumphs of the Christian faith—the martyr looking, like Stephen, into heaven with his dying eye; the agonies of Him who lived on earth in conflict that men might die in peace, and died in ignominy that men might live for ever in honor and joy; the sinless Mother looking with unutterable tenderness upon her infant God, her Saviour-Son, reposing in her arms, or looking with unutterable sorrow upon that Saviour-Son extended on the cross?

Would you devote yourselves to the ministrations of the Gospel? Find, then, in the priesthood work enough for any strength, patience enough for any discipline, order enough for any grace bestowed. Would you be martyrs to the faith? Know, then, that the days of martyrs are not yet over; you can become Catholic martyrs now, if you have that holy ambition. Within a few months Christian heroes and Christian heroines have died for their faith as firmly, as eagerly, as triumphantly as nearly two thousand years ago, by spires of flame kindled by mortal hate, Christian souls ascended to God, or fierce and roaring lions opened for them the gates of Paradise.

Will you devote your lives to deeds of mercy in asylums or hospitals? The Catholic Church has room enough for you. She has a hand to touch tenderly every woe, a word of consolation for every form of suffering. Nowhere, except in the Catholic Church, is so great ingenuity displayed to make so little do so much. Brotherhoods abound, in which you can labor and pray, and at the same moment, and by exactly the same work, serve the Lord of Glory and your fellow men. By patient toil and the grace of God you can make fields of grain to wave in the wilderness, and by patient toil and the grace of God you can make the more dreary wilderness of human souls to bloom and to bear the fruits of Christian penitence and joy. You can follow the plague in its terrible march with your touch—the royal touch of Heaven vouchsafed to you to heal souls, if not the withering frame. If war sounds its dreadful clangor, you can go upon the field to bear the wounded to a place of rest and care, or to bestow the last kindness which the living can render to the dead, breathing prayers for their souls while tenderly lifting their lifeless forms; all the while too busy in your work of love to mind the shrill rustling of the wings of death.

You gentler ones, how many sisterhoods there are in the Catholic Church designed to be friends of the friendless, to give hope to the hopeless, and help to the helpless, and a home to the homeless! How many patient sisters of how many orders are in the Catholic Church, ever eager, ever busy to heal or soothe all pains and maladies and woes and broken hearts! Behold the Sisters of Charity, whom even infidels who deny the existence of God or of angels will revere. Behold the Little Sisters of the Poor going from house to house to gather food for those in their charge—people who, as the world goes, have no claim upon them, but who, in their eyes, have a claim because they are in need. These sisters devote their lives to others, without regard to religion or race. It is enough for them to know that the afflicted ones for whom they care belong to the race of the helpless, and that they can recite the creed of the suffering.

Is there not room for Catholic self-denial, Catholic charity, Catholic loving-kindness in the nineteenth century as in the first century, when such qualities soothed as they now soothe the bitterness of life? The poor are with us, as Christ said they would be. Civilization has perils and troubles of its own. The Catholic Church has been the best friend of civilization, promoting its benefits, restraining its evils. Plagues yet wander over the earth; sin reigns in millions of hearts; sorrow invades every home. Is

there now no need, on earth, of the divine
rebukes, of the divine consolations of the
Catholic Church?

You whose only ambition is to be without ambition, even for holy service, if it
shall take you away from the quiet life of
home; who are content to serve God in
ways unseen of men; who, while faithful
and dutiful, draw back in terror from
the public eye, know, then, that the
Catholic Church abounds with meek and
faithful lives unrecognized by the world—
abounds, and yet there is room for more.
There is room for as many as will come, to
spend day after day, year after year,
praying, believing, toiling. Millions upon millions of Catholic Christians have
lived such lives, and have died in faith,
and are now in their celestial home.
They made no figure in the world. They
are not known in history. They shine not
out like stars which we can call by name
in the clear sky of night; but have you
not often seen that glorious white galaxy

that spans the sky when the great stars appear? In that galaxy of light no eye unaided can detect a single star. For many ages it was deemed a kind of perpetual cloudland, brilliant, mysterious, and beautiful. Science has to some degree solved the beautiful mystery, and has made it more beautiful still; for that galaxy of light is found to be made up of innumerable stars, no one of which the natural eye can discern, but which together, by their combined radiance, form the ethereal galaxy of night. So in Catholic history, millions of Catholic Christians, never known or heard of beyond the narrow circles of their homes, unrecognized as individuals in the records of men, nevertheless, by the combined beauty and brightness of their faithful lives and memories, circle the ages with a belt of light, as yonder galaxy, during the centuries that have been marching on since creation, has spanned and glorified the midnight sky. How many a beautiful soul, unknown on earth—perhaps, like its Redeemer, "despised and rejected of men"—now receives and gives immortal splendor in heaven's bright galaxy!

Why a Catholic in the nineteenth century? Because the scientific enquiries of the age need the directing hand of the Church. The Catholic Church has never been the foe of science; but she has always refused to treat scientific theories as established truths, and that, no doubt, she will continue to do. The Catholic Church acts in this way from her own divine instinct. She represents on earth immutable and eternal truth. How, then, can she, in faithfulness to her Divine Lord, venture to put, or permit to be put, the seal of immutable and eternal truth on theories which, however plausible or well supported, a few years may prove to be utterly unsound? When the scientific world is strewn with wrecks of theories, once apparently firm, strong, and durable, when all the natural sciences are avowedly adrift on an ocean of enquiry, why should the Catholic Church be blamed because she waits until any given theory becomes an incontrovertible truth before she sanctions it? Catholics equally ardent, equally faithful, have had different theories not only in natural science, but in moral and intellectual philosophy—different ways of explaining the laws of the universe of matter and of mind. The Catholic Church does not discourage human enquiry. She permits it and aids it, but she will not permit a theory, however plausible or probable, to be smuggled into the minds of men as Catholic truth. This is done not only for the proper care of the Church over her own prerogatives, but also for the interest and advancement of science.

What would be the result, as concerns science, if the Catholic Church should be eager to seal any new theory as Catholic truth, if a short time should upset the theory? Would not science lose more than she would gain, if the Catholic Church were ready to give her august sanction to unproved theories? That would stop investigation and enquiry. The Catholic Church, then, renders a true and great service to science by not impeding her widest, highest, deepest range, while protecting the Ark of God from assault and refusing to treat a theory as truth.

There is, however, so-called science, which the Catholic Church does not sanction. She refuses to it the name of science; and she cannot do otherwise. The first article of the Catholic Creed is this: "I believe in one God, the Father Almighty, Maker of Heaven and earth, of all things visible and invisible." This accords with the very first words of the Holy Scripture: "In the beginning God created heaven and earth." The Catholic Church regards that alone as having any right to be called science which makes it the undeniable axiom of all its investigations that all things were created, and, if created, they must have had a Creator. The Catholic Church has never recognized atheism as science, and it is very certain that she never will. An atheist is no more a man of science than a pagan is a Christian.

Admit the fact of creation, admit the existence of a Creator, and then and thence go as far as you will, soar as high as you will, go down as deep as you will, and the Catholic Church, so far from opposing your enquiries, will aid and encourage them, for she is the friend of learning of every kind; but in the nineteenth century there is with many a determination to regard science and atheism as convertible terms—or rather, atheism, arrayed in the robes of science, claims, by being so clad, immunity from censure and denunciation because pursuing scientific enquiries. The Catholic Church tears off the mask; she penetrates the disguise, she shows the impostor as he is, and then the atheistic monster, revealed in his native ugliness by the touch of the Ithuriel spear of Catholic truth, begins to howl and roar and rage, and to spit his venom against the Catholic Church as the foe of science.

For this reason, then, that the Catholic Church is, and ever will be, the defender of the truth that there is a God, and that all things, seen and unseen, all the powers of nature, all the laws of nature, are the work of his hands, she ought to be sustained by all sincere believers in the Christian faith. It is the duty, the binding duty, of these sincere believers to stand by the Catholic Church in this determined defence of that first principle of the truth of God—the existence of God; and the best way for a man to stand by the Catholic Church is to stand in the Catholic Church as one of her faithful and loving sons. The Ark of God is assailed in the nineteenth century with a bitterness, a subtle enmity—on one side by an hypocrisy, on another by a violence of attack—which no previous age has known. Formerly infidelity avowed itself to be infidelity, took the name, waved the flag, brought on the artilleries of infidelity. Now infidelity assumes the more pleasing and alluring name of science, and seeks to undermine those eternal towers of truth which for so many ages she has besieged without success.

Protestant believers in creation, in a Creator, this atheism in the garb of science claims you as its friends and allies. Are you willing to be so regarded ? Will you not, by joining your faith, your zeal, your love of God, your love of your Saviour Christ, ay, by joining yourselves to the Catholic Church, help her in upholding the truth of God, help her in resisting the enemies of God himself—those enemies who are trying to dethrone that very Being who breathed into them that breath of life which they spend in denying his existence or in scouting his authority ?

Why a Catholic in the nineteenth century ? Because there are great questions in morals, in the social relations of men, in the interwoven interests of capital and labor, in which the influence of the Catholic Church will be sure to be on the side of mercy, tenderness, justice, and impartial kindness towards all, even if not interfering by positive legislation. I have a right to believe that, on these great subjects, the influence of the Catholic Church will be on the side of equity, because it has been so, on the social questions of every age, since the beginning. The principles of the Catholic Church are unchangeable; but the applications of those principles are as various as the needs of men. As regards society and civilization, the influence of the Catholic Church has ever been in favor of the ascendency of law over brutal force, of freedom over slavery, of intellectual power over military power, of beneficent organization over anarchy and ruin.

Protestant scholars! will you not acknowledge that for centuries the might of the Catholic Church has been used to make souls, not swords, the rulers of the world—minds, not batteries, the sources of national power? Will you not acknowledge that in these respects she has won great victories?—though, of course, greater victories remain to be won; and these victories have been won by the patient, constant, unyielding efforts of ages, not by direct assault, but by pervading influence, by persuasion, by an incessant tendency to a higher individual and national life, not often by a direct use of the authority of the Church. The silent, almost unobserved, changes in society are alike the greatest and the most enduring. Compare the condition of laborers in all Christian countries with what it was in the days of the Roman Empire, and you will see the great result fulfilled; and the main author of that great change is the Catholic Church. A Roman laborer would not have believed it to be possible that in the course of time the position of laborers in society could be so greatly changed as it has been mainly by the influence of the Catholic Church. What has been the cause of this great change in society, so silent yet so effectual? Because the Catholic Church has ever felt that all men had souls—souls to be taught, to be warned, to be consoled, to be forgiven, to be approved or to be reproved—souls to be saved. She has taught the rich that their wealth could not save them. She has taught the poor that their poverty could not save them. To rich and poor she has taught that faith and obedience, on the human side of salvation, can alone save the souls of men. She has had but one doctrine, one baptism, one penitential discipline, one Eucharist, one benediction for the living, one prayer for the dying, one prayer for the dead, one religion—one religion, with all its rights and duties, alike for the laborer and the lord. One and the same baptism admits the child of the ploughman and the child of the king to her one and the same holy communion.

No human being is so low that she will not eagerly stoop, like the Divine Redeemer, to lift him up, if he is willing to be lifted. No human being is so high that she will not dare to drag him down, if he denies the rights of God or tramples on the souls for whom Christ died. The Catholic Church respects authority and law, and commands her children to respect them; but she asserts the equality of all men, as mortals needing the grace of God, and saved, if saved, by one and the same benignant Cross. The Catholic Church admits no royal road to salvation, but that road of sorrow which the King of kings trod with his weary feet on his way to crucifixion. The equality of men in their relation to God is a logical conclusion, if not an expressed doctrine, of the American Declaration of Independence; but that doctrine was preached by the Catholic Church for more than seventeen hundred years before the Declaration of Independence. It was the doctrine of the Sermon on the Mount. It was the doctrine of St. Paul. It was the doctrine expressly enforced on St. Peter in most evident reference to his headship in the Church of God.

In this doctrine is the very seal of the divine commission of the Catholic Church. Wrongs and oppressions have existed in the world, but not by the consent of the Catholic Church. How could slavery stand for ever against the influence of the Catholic Church? The slavery of race to race has been the law of the world from the beginning. No wrong was so deeply fixed in human history as that; yet the Catholic Church tore it out and broke it up in a great part of the world—not by violence, but by the still yet determined, incessant influence of ages. So only could be eradicated a wrong whose fibres penetrated every human institution and all human society. How could, how can the laborer be for ever trampled upon, while the Catholic Church incessantly affirms and defends the worth of human souls, as human souls, in the sight of God?

As it has been so it will be. The constant aim of the Catholic Church is to lift men up, and to keep them up, as immortal beings. That will be her aim, that will be the effect, of her teaching and guiding authority for ever.

The Catholic Church has ever regarded human life in the warm light of Christianity, not in the cold, dark, dreary shadow of political economy. "For the poor you have always with you." She has regarded these, the very words of Christ, as all the sanction she needs for her many systems of charity. Let me not be misunderstood. In a certain sphere and to a certain extent political economy is a true science; but when it goes beyond that sphere it becomes simply a masked battery for attacking the great principle of human brotherhood, which is the essential spirit of Christianity in its relation to the world. Political economy, like all the other sciences, is entitled to respect just so long as its course is guided by that north star in the sky of truth—the fact that all things were created and are under the guidance of a Creator. This fact, in relation to the social life of men, requires the admission of Christianity not only as historic truth, but as truth applicable, at all times and everywhere, to the changes of human need. When political economy denounces brotherly kindness as social crime, all forms of charity as subversive of civilization and order, as productive of dependence and indolence, and even dares to hint that it is best that the old and the feeble should be allowed, and even aided, to die for the general welfare, instead of being aided to live by Christian kindness; when it repeats its heartless words of supply and demand, of producer and consumer, to undermine the most ennobling emotions of the human heart and the most positive principles and precepts of the Christian faith, political economy becomes an apostate from true science and an enemy of God and man. Political economy becomes then not a friend of enlightened order and civil advancement, but the latest invention of the devil, to give, or to try to give, the sanctions of positive law to the spirit and practice of disobedience to the humane requirements of the Gospel of Christ.

The Catholic Church, then, by insisting always and everywhere upon the equality of men, as men, in the Christian dispensation, in their relation to God, having so far vastly improved the condition of the poor and the respect in which labor and the laborer are regarded, will not stop extending the same beneficent though, perhaps, silent influence. The Catholic Church has always repressed the spirit of agrarian outrages; she has defended invariably the rights of order and the rights of property; but her history for nearly two thousand years proves that it has been her constant aim, while directing man in his religious responsibilities, to improve his social condition; and this aim she has fulfilled. The people and popular rights have never had so true and persistent a friend as the Catholic Church. Look at the work of the Catholic Church in practical civilization, in clearing forests, in planting grain, in opening and developing new modes of honorable industry done by the monks of the Middle Ages, who set the example of faithful labor as an illustration of this truth. The Catholic Church believes in hard work —hard work of hands, hard work of heads; but she would make hard work more eagerly and cheerfully done, because inspired by holy aspirations. How much more men will do under the spur of lofty motives than when working in a slavish spirit! To give those lofty motives, to take away that slavish spirit, has been the aim, ay, it has been the effect, of the Catholic Church. The Catholic Church can sincerely urge people to work, for the good reason that the Catholic Church is herself the hardest worker under the sun.

Great questions, stormy questions, have arisen in the past in man's relation to the social order; and the Catholic Church has ever been ready to meet them and answer them fairly. The Catholic Church has ever upheld the principles of government and authority; but at the same time, by precept and example, she has favored justice in the spirit of kindness, and kindness in the spirit of justice, between man and man. It cannot be a mere coincidence, but it must be by some unseen influence, some mysterious and pervading sympathy, that, in all ages and in all lands, the Catholic Church, wherever she has found a home, has attracted and kept the earnest affection of the laboring, the striving, and the struggling, of those needing help, needing direction, needing consolation. This is not a coincidence. It is a logical and direct result of the divine presence with which she is endowed; it is the practical application of the commands of Christ her Lord. In these great social questions of the past the Catholic Church upheld law and authority; but she has also taught and demanded good-will for the oppressed and the afflicted. She will do the same again. She will win again, as she has won in the past, the appreciation of the friends of order and that of the friends of humanity. Great and grave questions in regard to capital and labor are appearing in gigantic proportions. These questions cannot be stifled or repressed by laws, however stringent. They cannot be answered by the hard heart and hard voice of political economy. Political economy, of itself, has never answered any great social question, and never will.

A man, then, who sees with dismay in the nineteenth century many and great problems, diverse perhaps in form, yet springing from the same root of earnest, striving manhood, and requiring one day to be settled, may be assured that the Catholic Church will be true to herself and her history. She will uphold authority; but she will tell law-makers, and she will tell them in a tone that will compel respect, that the men for whom they make laws have immortal souls; that they are not mere machines for increasing the profits of the rich and the grasping; that if one portion of the community must be restrained from breaking laws, another portion of the community must be restrained from breaking hearts. The Catholic Church teaches men to aspire to a higher life. She will try to open the way for their aspirations.

Why, then, a Catholic in the nineteenth century? Because in the great questions of social order and harmony the Catholic Church is needed, because the past has proved, and the present may, that she alone can have influence, just and impartial—severe it may be, in maintaining law, but equally just, impartial, and, if need be, severe in demanding that laws shall be merciful and humane. In those lands where the Catholic Church has never lost her ground, the poor and the striving have ever had for her the most loyal and devoted affection. In those lands where, by the treason of kings, the Catholic Church has lost her ground, the poor and the striving sigh for the times that are gone, when the poor and the striving were not deemed social outcasts, and treated as criminals, but when they were recognized as Christian brethren, when kind lips were eager to console them and kind hands were ready to help them.

Why a Catholic in the nineteenth century? Because the Catholic Church is not only the best friend of social order, based on reciprocal good-will, but she is the strongest defender of civil order—that is, of the state and of its institutions and laws. A man high in authority recently uttered a sentiment which good citizens of all kinds of political views hailed with assent and delight. It was this: "He serves his party best who serves his country best." Now, while most cordially approving that sentiment as worthy to be a political axiom, I venture to go one step beyond and to say, He serves his country best who best serves Christ and the Church. And by the Church I mean the Catholic Church. I am not going to enter into the great subject of the relation of the Church of Christ to civil authority. That is no doubt the great subject of the times; but it is too large to be treated here as it deserves. It is enough for the present to state a few plain truths. If Christ founded a Church —and it is admitted that he did—and if that Church is an institution, as it must be if intended to survive our Lord's earthly life, and since it has so survived, then it would be impossible that such an institution should not be felt as a new and great power in the world, not only by its influence on individual minds, but on civil society. That has been the fact; and if Christ was, as we believe, God incarnate, that must have been designed to be the fact; for it is impossible that an Infinite

Being should have established on earth an institution, having a supernatural life, that should not be a constant incentive to higher life both to men and nations, a constant warning and protest against ignoble aims in men and nations. Those who call that ascendency of the Church in all human affairs a usurpation must be blind to the real nature of the Church. Does right, when triumphant, usurp the place of wrong? Does a great statesman usurp the place of a little statesman, if momentous public emergencies have brought him to the place of power, superseding inferior merit? Is the love of holiness, when it gains and keeps a victory in a soul which has hitherto loved sin, guilty of a usurpation? Is Christ himself a usurper when he reigns in hearts which have hitherto been devoted to Satan? If it be so, it is a most blessed usurpation, and may God fill the world with such acts of usurpation! Then would indeed the New Jerusalem descend to earth.

The Catholic Church was designed to pervade by her influence all the affairs of men. There is no usurpation in this. It is her divine prerogative. This is no strained conclusion. It follows from the admission that Christ is divine, that he founded a Church which should represent him and be endowed by his life; and such an institution could not be on the earth, and be in any way or degree faithful to itself and its Lord, without profoundly and widely impressing all divine interests and all human interests; and this influence it would have not by accident, not by caprice, not merely by entreaty, but by right, and, if by right, then necessarily by divine right; for a divine institution cannot have any organic rights that are not divine. The fact is, no doubt, historical that in very many cases the intervention of the Church was earnestly invited and sought in the affairs of nations; and the Church complied with the invitation and soothed enmities, established peace, and made the right victorious; but it is an overturn of the truth to say that the right so to make peace and establish justice came from the invitation and entreaty. On the contrary, the invitation and entreaty came from the right and the conviction of the right in the minds of those who sought and invited aid. The Church has no right to turn aside from her divine mission to do anything anywhere under the pressure of any invitation or entreaty, however urgent; and she has not broken this rule, as shallow thinkers accuse her of doing many times, when what she has done, though in answer to the most earnest solicitation, has been nevertheless in accord with her divine commission. If the whole world is to be converted to Christ, it is difficult to see how human governments can be for ever alienated from Christ.

So far with general principles. Now, what is the nature of this influence of the Church? It is to build up, not to destroy; to refine and purify, not to debase; it is to teach man, whether as an individual or a citizen, to love God, to serve God, to be just and true in all the relations of life. Is there anything in this influence subversive of civil rights ? Is the man who tries to act daily in the faith and fear of God, as the Catholic Church tells him to act, a bad citizen; while the man who cares nothing for God, even if he condescends to admit his existence, and who makes it his boast to do nothing, if he can help it, which the Catholic Church approves, and to do everything which he can that the Catholic Church condemns, a good citizen, a preeminently good citizen—in fact, the only good citizen ?

Why, then, a Catholic in the nineteenth century ? Because the governments of the world, even of Christendom, have held very lightly their Christian responsibilities, and they need that sustaining yet elevating and ennobling influence which the Catholic Church can impart, and which was never more needed in the history of the world than in the year of our Lord 1877.

The Catholic Church and the nations of the earth can develop their respective powers in perfect harmony. There is no need of any jar, of any contradiction, of any jealousy. The stronger the nations are, the stronger the Catholic Church must be; and the stronger the Catholic Church is, the stronger the nations may safely be. This is not an age of faith, but it ought to be—if for no other reason, simply in gratitude to the Church of Christ; for that very materialism which is the most marked characteristic of the age is a distortion and misdirection of those capabilities which the Catholic Church has developed in men by her constant attention not only to spiritual life, not only to intellectual progress, but to practical civilization. The revival of learning and of art, which is often claimed as a reaction against Catholic influence, was just the reverse, being the result of Catholic influence in widening and deepening the minds of men for centuries, preparing even barbarians to appreciate the ancient culture; and so the appliances of human discovery and invention for the comfort, refinement, and elevation of communities are but the continuation through Protestant conditions of the spirit of enterprise and civilizing energy which had a Catholic source. But there is this difference: in Catholic times and in Catholic nations what may be called practical civilization was held in subjection to the higher life of men and of nations. It was a way to a goal, and that goal a more refined and a nobler manhood; but in Protestant times and in Protestant countries this practical civilization, this result of inventions and discoveries, is regarded as the very goal of enlightenment, an object to be sought for itself, as the ultimate aim of social and national life. Hence materialism in society and in philosophy becomes itself a standard, and, of course, a false standard, of civilization. The Catholic Church has never opposed enterprise. She is herself, laying aside all divine claims, the most enterprising society that the world ever knew ; but she has sought to direct and regulate enterprise, that it may not bring all the higher and nobler faculties of men and nations into subjection to degrading aims and worldly success. For a thousand years nations were great exactly in proportion as they were inspired by Catholic ardor and devoted to the welfare and extension of the Catholic Church.

Why, then, a Catholic in the nineteenth century ? Because there is a special need that the materialism which practical civilization, uninspired by Catholic truth and Catholic traditions, has brought upon human society should be so directed that it may no longer be an end but a means of advancement. Now, what are nations but people, and people having souls ? The Catholic Church aims to elevate the souls of people, and just so far as she does this she elevates the nations. When all people shall be converted to Christ, of course, all nations will be converted to Christ; and when that result shall come, or even when it shall be near, all the charges and jealousies about the relations of the Catholic Church to civil authority and human progress will vanish into air. Then statesmen and scholars, philosophers and patriots, will be eager to enquire not how little but how much of national law, of civil authority, of enterprise, of science and art, of all the social, secular, and religious energy of man, shall be consecrated to Christ and the Church, and consequently consecrated by Christ and the Church.

Why a Catholic in the nineteenth century? Because the age needs to be inspired by an ardent faith in Christ. Most heartily do I admit that many persons outside the body of the Catholic Church have a sincere and ardent faith in Christ. They are ignorant of the divine beauty of the Catholic Church, or, very likely, they would be eager to kneel at her altar, to receive her sacramental seals. The nineteenth century needs Christian fervor, Christian zeal, Christian enthusiasm, Christian energy. The Catholic Church has been a Church, as her enemies admit, of intense and never-ending activity. She incites and arouses the hearts of her children as no other organization claiming to be a church has begun to show; yet the Catholic Church, while herself so ardent, even, if you will, so impetuous and aggressive in her advance, distrusts ardor and enthusiasm outside her fold. She admits the good faith of many whose modes of activity she cannot wholly approve. Why is this? There seems to be 'an inconsistency here. I admit it, but will try to explain it. Religious emotion, even Christian emotion, outside the Catholic Church is adrift, without compass, pilot, or rudder. When there is nothing to hold on by, nothing to hold on to, enthusiasm, even if it be of religious intention, is very dangerous, as history has often proved. Some of the fiercest outbreaks of human passion have had an origin in religious emotion, but religious emotion undirected. Religious ardor, misguided, has often driven men into wild excesses and made wrecks of human souls. The Catholic Church can safely incite religious emotion to ardor, even to vehemence, because she is founded on a rock—on the rock of eternal truth. Religious emotion in the Catholic Church is the fragrant, blooming flower of Catholic faith. It is not a transient feeling springing up on the occasion, and perhaps dying with it; or, if not, it may be resulting in devastation of hearts and minds, of the whole intellectual and spiritual nature. Catholic emotion obeys the compass, the rudder, the pilot of immutable truth. It is not adrift upon a boiling ocean of religious frenzy. If natural science were a positive thing, and not a congregation of theories—some probable, some possible, and some improbable, if not impossible—

we could say with truth that what principles are to science dogmas are to the religious nature. The illustration will but partially suit. Guided and guarded by the dogmas of the Catholic Church, the Catholic preacher can speak with the utmost fervor; and the Catholic hearer can safely permit his soul to be moved and inspired by the earnest words, for the Catholic preacher in his most impassioned oratory will but urge his hearer to be true to the unchanging faith of Christ and to live according to it; and the Catholic hearer can rightly obey the impulse, because in the very eagerness of his devotion he is required to hold with a firmer grasp substantial truth.

Now, the nineteenth century needs a powerful reaction against the sordid materialism which spreads so far and goes down so deep, weakening, if not poisoning, the very roots of individual, social, and national life The nineteenth century pre-eminently needs enthusiasm—intense, pervading, exulting enthusiasm—to lift it out of its grovelling track. It needs a strong, persistent, spiritual impulse. The nineteenth century needs voices and souls impassioned, even on fire, with religious zeal. The Catholic Church alone can supply the need. She alone, through the grace of God, can give to the soul wings to soar and to keep a sustained, unbroken flight. The Catholic Church alone can wisely kindle the fires of religious feeling, because those fires under her care become ministrant to human consolation and not sources of ruin and waste. The Catholic Church can lead her children into the valley of humiliation or up the height of joy, because in that valley Catholic penitence and Catholic faith keep the hands of the soul that it may not fall into despair, and on the height of joy Catholic wisdom can be near to prevent the soul being torn and blasted by the rugged and volcanic ridges of spiritual pride. Why, then, a Catholic in the nineteenth century? Because the nineteenth century needs to be drawn away by some mighty power from ignoble aims and objects, and that mighty power can alone be found on earth in the Catholic Church.

Why a Catholic in the nineteenth century? Because this age needs for its own sake to appreciate the lofty examples of Christian heroism which fill the past ages with glory. The age is material, sordid, and mercantile. It needs the infusion of spiritual chivalry—the adherence to right aims against all difficulties and in the face of all foes. This spirit of holy chivalry survives on earth only in the Catholic Church and in her influence outside her pale. The present age is not lacking in sublime examples of this holy Christian chivalry. There is one most illustrious instance, and it is found, as might be expected, in the Catholic Church. How greatly would it console every thoughtful Christian who loves and tries to serve the Church of Christ if all the world could or would duly estimate the heroic endurance, the supernatural serenity born of faith and patience, the cheerful and undoubting hope, which are the special characteristics of that grand and venerable man who, in the city of Rome, the metropolis of Christendom, presides over the Church of God. Let the nineteenth century stand and revere that noble example of the power of the Church to inspire a spirit that can defy wrongs and injuries—calm, confident, triumphant in soul, even when oppressed by the malignity of men, proving that God rules, that trials are but milestones in the holy progress of the Church, and signs of her unfailing loyalty; proving also that God will in his own time give to right and patience the victory.

How vastly moral and spiritual grandeur excels the grandeur of nature! How grand is Chimborazo, rising in majesty a king of mountains! How grand is Niagara, with its eternal roar and eternal motion! But a true Christian hero is the grandest spectacle which time can show. Since, then, spiritual sublimity so far exceeds the sublimity of nature, we have a right to believe that the most sublime object now on this earth in the sight of God and of the hosts of heaven is Pope Pius the Ninth. Permit me to cite a few lines which I wrote before becoming a Catholic, yet having in my mind while writing them the example of the noblest hero of the nineteenth century—Pius the Ninth :

> What should he care for mortal might,
>   The scorner's jeer, the tyrant's rod,
> Who holds his ground, maintaining right,
>   Armed with the eternal truth of God?
> Why should he swerve, or quail, or quiver
> At sight of chains or death's cold river?
> Those very chains the proof may be
> His soul is truly brave and free,
> And death's cold river may begin
> Triumphant life which martyrs win.

www.ingramcontent.com/pod-product-compliance
Lightning Source LLC
Chambersburg PA
CBHW021948160426
43195CB00011B/1269